LET'S VISIT...

LONDON

Annabelle Lynch

W

FRANKLIN WATTS

LONDON · SYDNEY

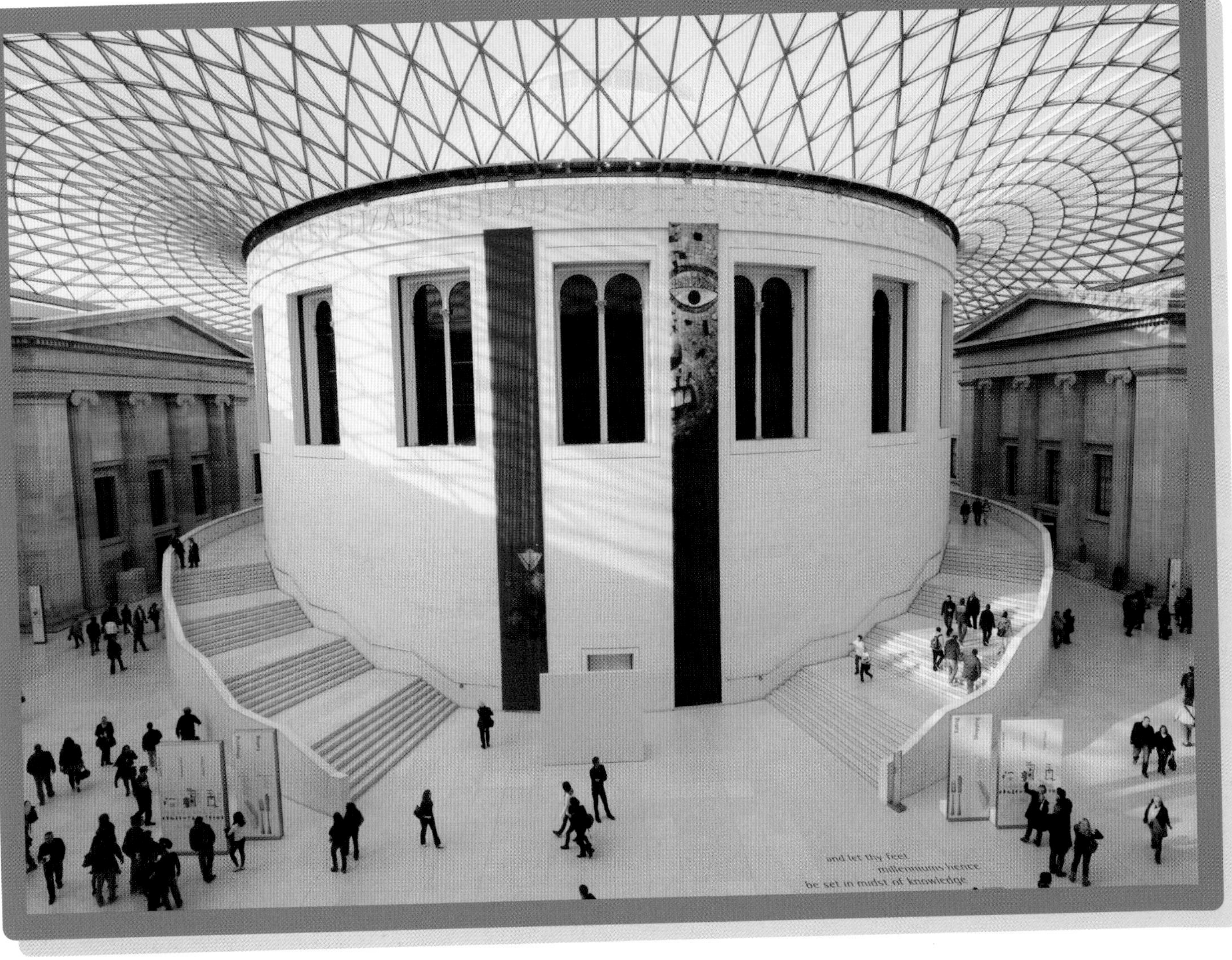

Franklin Watts
Published in Great Britain in 2017
by the Watts Publishing Group

Editor: Sarah Silver
Designer: D.R. ink

HB ISBN 978 1 4451 5365 0
PB ISBN 978 1 4451 5366 7

Printed in China

Photo acknowledgements:
allylondon/Shutterstock: 20t. Natalia
Antonova/Shutterstock: 7b. Aurinko/
Dreamstime: 26b. Roger Bacon/Reuters/
Alamy: 29bl. Tony Baggett/istockphoto:
18-19. Peter Barritt/Superstock: 10br. Dan
Breckwoldt/Dreamstime: 2, 22. David Cole/
Alamy: 23b. Piero Crucuatti/Alamy: 11b.
Mark Cuthbert/Getty Images: 24c. Ian
Dagnall/Alamy: 7t, 29cr. Veryan Dale/
Alamy: 21b. Songquan Deng/Shutterstock:
4-5. Chris Dorney/Shutterstock: 14-15.
Tony French/Alamy: 8b. Jeff Gilbert/
Alamy: 28-29c. GL Archive/Alamy: 12cl.
Tom Hanley/Alamy: 7c.Neville Mountford-
Hoare/Alamy: 19c. Holgs/istockphoto:
12t. Anton Ivanov/Shutterstock: 3bc,16.
Slawek Kozakiewicz/Dreamstime: 24b.
Mark Lange/ANL/REX/Shutterstock: 25.
Neil Lange/Shutterstock: 15c, 15b. Peter
Lovas/Dreamstime: 8t. Herbert Mason/
Everett Historical/Shutterstock: 4c.
Lucan Milican/Shutterstock: 5t. Dmitry
Naumov/Shutterstock: 3br, 10bl. Kapi Ng/
Shutterstock: 5c. Pawel Pajor/Shutterstock:
26-27. John Pavel/Dreamstime: 13. Plus
One/Shutterstock: 17t. rabbit75_ist/
istockphoto: front cover. Eugene Regis/
Shutterstock: 11t. Ray Roberts/Alamy: 9.
Guido Alberto Rossi/AGF/Alamy: 28b.
Mikhail Sh/Shutterstock: 27b. Henrik
Stovring/Dreamstime: 21t.
Think Design Manage/Dreamstime: 1, 6.
Ileana-Marcela Bosogea-Tudor/
Dreamstime: 27t. Kiev Victor/Shutterstock:
20b. VPC Travel/Alamy: 17b. Martin Zak
Dreamstime: 23t.

Franklin Watts
An Imprint of
Hachette Children's Books
Part of the Watts Publishing Group
Carmelite House
50 Victoria Embankment
London EC4Y 0DZ

An Hachette UK Company
www.hachette.co.uk
www.franklinwatts.co.uk

CONTENTS

Words in **bold** are in the glossary.

LET'S VISIT
LONDON

Welcome to the great city of London! London is England and the United Kingdom's capital city. It is in the south-east of England.

Historic place

London has a long and exciting history, which stretches back nearly two thousand years. Over the centuries, London and its people have survived **invasions**, huge fires and wars.

London was badly bombed during the Second World War (1939-1945). →

Lots to see and do

Today, London is one of the biggest and most famous cities in the world. Millions of people visit it every year to see its great museums, parks and art **galleries**.

Tourists sit outside The National Gallery (see page 10).

TOP TIP

Children and young people up to the age of 18 can apply for a Zip Oyster card. This gives free or discounted travel around London.

Time to travel

The quickest way to get around London is on the London Underground (or Tube). It's the oldest underground railway system in the world! If you have more time, you can hop on a famous red London bus (above) or a Thames ferry. But the best way to see many of London's sights is on foot.

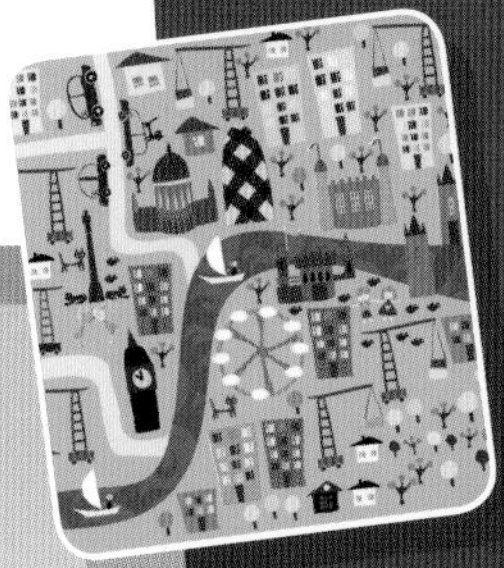

THE TOWER OF LONDON

The Tower of London sits beside the River Thames.

Discover London's exciting, and sometimes scary, past at the Tower of London.

TOP TIP

Download the Time Explorers app to explore the Tower, complete challenges and win badges.

Power tower

The Tower of London was built in the 11th century by the new king, William the Conqueror (ruled 1066–1087). He built it to keep him safe and show his power over London and the rest of England. Over the centuries, different kings and queens added new buildings around the first tower. It was used as a palace, an **armoury** and a home for the Royal **Mint**.

Anne Boleyn
(c. 1501–1536)

From palace to prison

Most famously, the Tower was used as a prison for enemies of the kings and queens of England. During the **reign** of Henry VIII (ruled 1491–1547), many important people were kept prisoner here. These included Anne Boleyn, the second wife of King Henry VIII. Her ghost is said to haunt the Tower!

The Crown Jewels

There are lots of things to see at the Tower, but the Crown Jewels are the most famous. Highlights include St Edward's Crown, which has been used at the **coronation** of every English king or queen since the 17th century, and Cullinan I, the largest clear diamond in the world.

St Edward's Crown (top) and the Imperial State Crown are part of the Crown Jewels.

DON'T MISS

The spooky black ravens – guardians of the Tower. It is said that if they ever leave, the Tower and the kingdom itself will lose all its power.

7

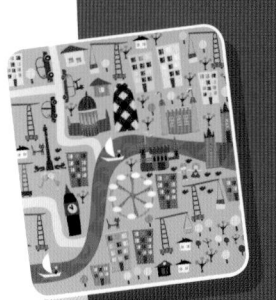

THE LONDON TRANSPORT MUSEUM

London is a big, busy city. Find out about its important transport systems at the London Transport Museum.

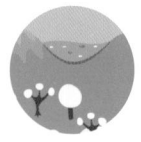

From road to rail

The London Transport Museum lets you experience what it would have been like to travel around London two hundred years ago. Jump on an old horse-drawn bus, ring the bell on a tram or hitch a ride on the very first electrical underground train. Around the museum, actors in historical dress help bring London's past to life.

Step inside an old London Underground train.

TOP TIP

The museum is in the heart of London's busy Covent Garden. Look out for the funny street performers!

Time for play

At the All Aboard play zone you can make your own driver announcements, help to repair a broken-down Tube train, find people's lost things at the Lost Property Office or have a go at busking with some musical instruments! If you're feeling a bit tired after all that work, take a break at the museum café, where you can have a refreshing Tube line milkshake.

↑ Don't forget to pick up a ticket to ride on the tram!

DON'T MISS
The Tube driving simulator, where you can guide your own train around London's busy underground network.

THE NATIONAL GALLERY AND THE TATE MODERN

Get into art at two of London's best art galleries.

Famous collection

The National Gallery (below) brings together over two thousand works of art from the 13th to the 20th centuries. It's a great place to see some of the world's most famous paintings, such as Vincent van Gogh's *Sunflowers*. At weekends and during school holidays, there are workshops to let you create art for yourself.

Sunflowers, Vincent van Gogh (1888)

TOP TIP

Download and print out a National Gallery trail at www.nationalgallery. org.uk to bring with you on your visit. Each trail highlights five important paintings and tells the story behind them.

The Turbine Hall at the Tate Modern is home to giant works of art.

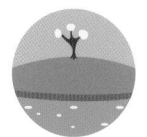

Starting with art

The Tate Modern building itself is impressive – an old **power station** on the bank of the River Thames. Inside, you can explore an amazing and sometimes surprising collection of art from the 20th and 21st centuries, including paintings, prints, **sculptures** and videos.

Get involved

Make the most of a trip to the Tate Modern with the free pick-up activities, which will get you thinking about the art you see in a new way. At the end of your visit, make some art for yourself at the digital drawing bar (left).

DON'T MISS

A visit to the viewing platform at the top of the Tate Modern, which gives fantastic views over London.

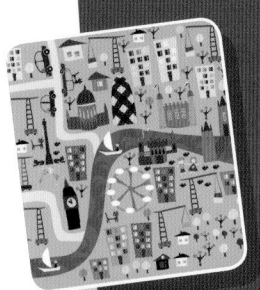

ST PAUL'S AND THE MONUMENT

St Paul's Cathedral is one of the most famous sights in London, if not the world.

A great fire

St Paul's Cathedral has stood in the heart of London for over 1,400 years. It hasn't always looked the same, though. In September 1666 a great fire spread through London, destroying thousands of buildings. St Paul's Cathedral was burned to the ground.

In 1666, the Great Fire of London raged through London for four days.

DON'T MISS

The Whispering Gallery in St Paul's, where a whisper can be heard on the other side of the cathedral dome – over 30 m away!

Climb the cathedral

Sir Christopher Wren (1632–1723) designed the cathedral we see today between 1675 and 1710. Today, you can climb the 528 steps up to the Golden Gallery and enjoy amazing views over London (when you get your breath back!). Or, if you're feeling brave, visit the **crypt** underneath St Paul's, where famous men, including the war hero Lord Nelson, and Wren himself, are buried.

A lasting monument

Close to St Paul's is the mighty Monument to the Great Fire of London (above). It stretches 61 m up into the sky – the distance between the Monument and the bakery where the fire first began – and is topped with an urn of golden flames. You can climb 311 steps to the viewing gallery.

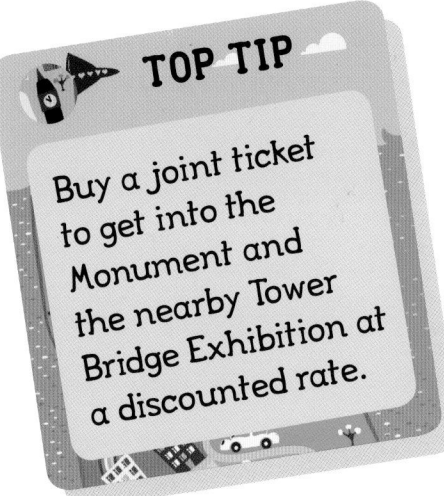

TOP TIP

Buy a joint ticket to get into the Monument and the nearby Tower Bridge Exhibition at a discounted rate.

THE QUEEN ELIZABETH OLYMPIC PARK

> Get active at the fantastic Queen Elizabeth Olympic Park.

 London 2012

In the summer of 2012, London hosted the Olympic and Paralympic Games. Over four weeks of exciting sporting action thrilled the world, as top athletes battled it out to win gold, silver and bronze medals.

 Swim, cycle, bat

Many new facilities were built for the games. Today, anyone can use these at the Queen Elizabeth Olympic Park. Splash in the 50-m swimming pool at the Aquatics Centre, have a go at badminton or basketball at the Copper Box Arena or tackle the mountain biking or BMX courses on your bike.

Tumble about

To the north of the park, the Tumbling Bay playground is a great place to get active and have fun. There are rockpools to splash in, wobbly bridges to cross, ropes to swing from and treehouses to explore. Make sure you visit the Pleasure Gardens, where you can dig and build in the enormous sandpit or have a go at the climbing wall.

TOP TIP

Bring a picnic to enjoy the park's lovely surroundings and busy wildlife.

Have fun digging in the park's sandpits.

DON'T MISS

The maze of 195 fountains, which is lit up with beautiful colours at night.

15

THE SCIENCE MUSEUM

Celebrate the world of science at the amazing Science Museum.

Visit the Energy Hall to find out about the history of steam power.

Great inventions

The Science Museum first opened its doors in 1857. It now brings together over 300,000 different objects from the world of science, from Puffing Billy – the oldest surviving **steam locomotive** – to the Clock of the Long Now, which is designed to keep ticking for 10,000 years!

DON'T MISS

The real-life command module from the Apollo 10 mission to the moon.

Space age

Galleries in the museum have different topics, such as flight, medicine and digital technology. One of the most exciting galleries is all about space. Here, you can discover the history of space exploration, from the first space missions to man's visits to the moon, right up to today's Mars **rovers**.

Hands-on fun

The museum is packed full of interactive exhibits to bring science to life. Try the Pattern Pod, where you can make ripples in a **virtual** pool, create your own digital picture, or project a puzzle onto the ceiling as you build it. For younger children, the Garden has giant blocks to build with and a huge water table.

You can play with colourful plasma balls like these at the Science Museum.

HMS BELFAST

Get shipshape! Visit HMS *Belfast* on the River Thames.

World at war

HMS *Belfast* is a Royal Navy warship. It played an important part in the Second World War. It protected supply ships and supported soldiers during the Normandy Landings in June 1944, which helped lead Britain and its **allies** to victory.

DON'T MISS
The interactive Operations Room where you can pretend to take part in a real–life naval rescue mission.

All aboard!

HMS *Belfast* was retired from service in 1963 and has been kept on the Thames in London since 1971. Visit it to discover what life at sea was really like for the 950 crew who lived aboard for months at a time. You can explore the rooms where the sailors slept, ate, washed their clothes and visited the sick bay or dentist. Dotted around the ship are models, stories of real-life sailors and exciting activities to help you get the most out of your visit.

 TOP TIP

Look out for nearby Tower Bridge (below) lifting up to let boats pass underneath. The bridge is raised around 1,000 times a year.

You can visit the control deck of HMS *Belfast* – and pretend to be the captain!

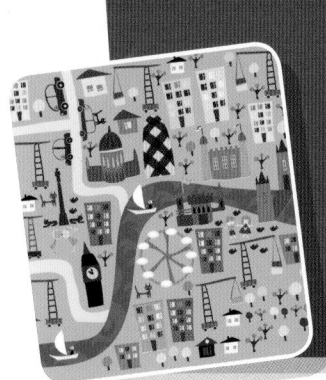

KEW GARDENS

Discover some of the world's most beautiful plants at London's Kew Gardens.

Glorious gardens

The Temperate House greenhouse dates back to 1859.

Kew Gardens first opened over 250 years ago, in 1759. Today it is spread over 1.2 km^2 of spectacular gardens and woodlands with huge glasshouses, lily ponds, sculpture trails and much more to see. The plants change with the seasons, so the gardens can look different from visit to visit.

The Palm House is home to exotic plants from around the world.

Treetop thrills

Kew's beautiful arboretum has over 2,000 different types of tree to see. Take it all in by climbing up to the famous Treetop Walkway and follow it as it winds for 200 m in the treetops. Have fun afterwards in the Treetop Towers playground!

Get up close with the tallest trees on the 18-m-high Treetop Walkway.

DON'T MISS

The fascinating Marine Aquarium where you can see the plants of four water habitats – coral reefs, rocky shores, estuaries and mangrove swamps.

Busy bees and badgers

Learn more about the relationship between plants and animals and how they work together in Kew's fun, interactive activities. Visit the busy honeybees in the Bee Garden, hide away in a badger sett or spot an **endangered** stag beetle in the loggery.

Discover what a badger's home is really like in the human-sized badger sett.

THE BRITISH MUSEUM

Explore mankind's eventful history at the famous British Museum.

The Great Court inside the museum has the Reading Room at its centre.

From past to present

The British Museum was the world's first museum when it opened over 250 years ago. Today its incredible collections feature over eight million objects spanning nearly two million years of human history, from a 1.8-million-year-old stone chopping tool to **solar-powered** lamps from the 21st century.

Highlights

There is so much to see at the museum that you might get a bit tired! Make sure you find the magnificent mummies in the ancient Egypt display, the Anglo-Saxon treasures from the Sutton Hoo ship burial and the world's most famous chess set, the Lewis Chessmen, which dates back to Viking times.

DON'T MISS

The Rosetta Stone. The writing on this ancient stone helped people to unlock the mystery of Egyptian hieroglyphs.

 The Lewis Chessmen are made from walrus ivory and whales' teeth.

Follow the trail

Get the most from a trip to the British Museum by picking up one of the six explorer trails booklets. These will take you on a journey of discovery around the museum, challenging you to really look at the exhibits to uncover fascinating stories of the past.

LONDON ZOO

Go wild with the animals at London Zoo!

Amazing creatures

A trip to London Zoo is essential for animal spotting. One of the oldest zoos in the world, it has a collection of over 17,000 different animals, from tiny leafcutter ants to burly gorillas. The animals' surroundings are as similar as possible to their home in the wild.

The zoo's gorillas live in a big enclosure that has an indoor gym and an island!

DON'T MISS
The Land of the Lions, where you can take part in an interactive lion rescue adventure.

Let a ring-tailed coati sit on your knee in the Tree Top Zone.

In with the animals

You can get up close with many of the animals. Watch the busy spiders at work in the walk-through spider exhibit, take a stroll through the lemur forest or let a beautiful butterfly land on your shoulder! You can also watch many of the animals being fed, including the fierce big cats.

Protecting wildlife

London Zoo works hard to help save animals in the wild. It is also home to some of the rarest and most endangered creatures in the world. Look out for the pygmy hippos, the white-naped mangabey monkeys and the very endangered Chinese giant salamander.

THE NATURAL HISTORY MUSEUM

Discover the wonders of the natural world at the Natural History Museum.

Colour coded

The Natural History Museum holds a mindboggling 80 million **specimens** of plants, insects, animals and **minerals**. There are four zones to make it easier to find what you want to see. The blue zone looks at **mammals**, dinosaurs, fish and reptiles, while the green zone explores plants, birds and the **environment**. The wildlife gardens and Darwin Centre are part of the orange zone, and the red zone is all about volcanoes, earthquakes and planet Earth.

Come face to face with a terrifying T-Rex!

See hundreds of specimens inside the Cocoon including beetles, butterflies and huge spiders.

Highlights

The Natural History Museum is most famous for its collection of dinosaur models, but there are lots of other amazing things to see and do. Look up in the entrance hall and you will see the 25-m-long skeleton of a blue whale – the biggest mammal on Earth. Feel the ground beneath you shake in the earthquake simulator and gaze in wonder at the millions of plant and insect specimens in the Cocoon (above).

DON'T MISS

The fossil of an archaeopteryx. This 147-million-year-old creature had feathers like a bird, but teeth, claws and a tail like a dinosaur.

THE MUSEUM OF LONDON

London itself is the star at the Museum of London.

Through the ages

The Museum of London is the very best place to discover the fascinating history of London and its people. It tells London's story from **prehistoric** times before London was even built, to its growth under Roman rule, its journey through Saxon, medieval and Victorian times, right up to the 21st century.

The Lord Mayor's coach is used at the Lord Mayor's Show every November.

Best bits

The museum has nine galleries and over six million exhibits, so there is plenty to see! Look out for a 200,000-year-old mammoth jaw that was found in modern-day Essex, some cheeky Roman graffiti, toys from the 17th century and a 110-year-old London taxi. You should also try to see the grand Lord Mayor's coach (above), which is still used today.

Get involved

Snuggle up in a model Saxon cottage, fetch water to help put out the flames of the Great Fire of London, experience the Blitz in the Second World War interactive exhibit or window-shop in a Victorian street.

You can see old bottles and jars of medicine at the Victorian pharmacy.

DON'T MISS
The huge copper cauldron, which lit up the London 2012 Olympic ceremony.

29

MAP OF LONDON

KEY:

1 London Zoo
2 St Paul's Cathedral
3 Monument
4 The British Museum
5 The London Transport Museum
6 Queen Elizabeth Olympic Park
7 The Tower of London

8 HMS *Belfast*
9 The Tate Modern
10 The National Gallery
11 The Museum of London
12 The Science Museum
13 The Natural History Museum
14 Kew Gardens

GLOSSARY

allies
Countries that fight together on the same side during a war

armoury
A place where weapons are kept

command module
The control centre of a spacecraft

coronation
The ceremony at which a king or queen is crowned

crypt
An room underneath a cathedral or church

endangered
At risk of dying out

environment
The natural world

fossil
The traces in rock of animals or plants that lived millions of years ago

gallery
A room or building where works of art or objects are displayed

habitat
The place where an animal or plant is usually found in the wild

hieroglyphs
A writing system using pictures; used in ancient Egypt

invasion
When an army enters a country by force

mammal
A creature with hair that gives birth to babies and feeds them with their own milk

mineral
A substance that is formed naturally in rocks and in the earth

mint
The place where a country's money is made

power station
A place where electricity is made

prehistoric
The period of time before people learned how to write things down

reign
The period of time that a king or queen rules a country

rover
A remote-controlled vehicle used to explore remote places

sculpture
A work of art that is made by shaping materials such as stone, metal or wood

simulator
A machine that lets you experience what it would be like to do something

solar-powered
Fuelled by the energy of the Sun

specimen
A single example of an animal or plant

steam locomotive
An engine powered by steam that pulls a train along the track

virtual
An object or activity created by a computer to give the experience of the real object or activity

INDEX

FURTHER INFORMATION

Books

My London Infographic Sticker Activity Book by Kay Barnham (Wayland, 2016)

L is for London by Paul Thurlby (Hodder Children's Books, 2015)

Websites

www.visitengland.com/things-to-do/london

www.visitlondon.com

www.timeout.com/london/things-to-do